Footballers

Tracey Turner

EDGE
FRANKLIN WATTS

First published in 2014 by
Franklin Watts
338 Euston Road
London NW1 3BH

Franklin Watts Australia
Level 17/207 Kent Street
Sydney NSW 2000

Text © Tracey Turner 2013
Design © Franklin Watts 2013

Series editor: Adrian Cole
Editor: Paul Rockett
Art direction: Peter Scoulding
Design: D R Ink
Picture research: Diana Morris

Acknowledgements:
Action Press/Rex Features: 23.
AFP/Getty Images: 18.
Back Page Images/Rex Features: 20.
Central Press/Hulton Archive/Getty Images: 16.
Coloursport/Corbis: 17.
Gerry Cranham/Offside/Rex Features: 22.
Stuart Franklin/Bongarts/Getty Images: 1, 6.
Getty Images: 5, 8. Hulton Archive/Getty Images: 13.
Paul Keevil/Actionplus/Topfoto: 19.
Offside Sports Photography: 21. PA Photos/Topfoto: 14.
Joern Pollex/Bongarts/Getty Images: 7.
Popperfoto/Getty Images: 11.
Christo Prudnaya/Shutterstock: front cover b, back cover t.
Real Madrid via Getty Images: 9.
Rolls Press/Popperfoto/Getty Images: 15.
Shaw/Associated Newspapers/Rex Features: 12.
George Tiedmann/Corbis: 4.
Bob Thomas/Getty Images: front cover t, 10.

A CIP catalogue record for this book
is available from the British Library.

Dewey Classification: 796.3'34'00922

(pb) ISBN: 978 1 4451 1474 3
(Library ebook) ISBN: 978 1 4451 2511 4

Printed in China

Franklin Watts is a division of Hachette
Children's Books, an Hachette UK company.
www.hachette.co.uk

**Warning!
This is not a
normal book!**

Contents

Please note: every effort has been made by the Publishers to ensure that
the websites in this book contain no inappropriate or offensive material.
However, because of the nature of the Internet, it is impossible to
guarantee that the contents of these sites will not be altered. We strongly
advise that Internet access is supervised by a responsible adult.

* These statistics were correct at the time this book was printed, but
because of the nature of football, it cannot be guaranteed that they
are now accurate.

Ultimate 20 is not just a book where you can find out loads of facts and stats about fantastic stuff – it's also a brilliant game book!

How to play

1. Grab a copy of *Ultimate 20* – oh, you have. OK, now get your friends to grab a copy, too.

2. Each player closes their eyes and flicks to a game page. Now, open your eyes and choose one of the Ultimate 20. Decide who goes first, then that person reads out the name of the footballer they've chosen, plus the name of the stat. For example, this player has chosen Lionel Messi and the Date of Birth stat, with an Ultimate 20 ranking of 1.

Date of birth: 24/06/87   **1**
Club goals: 226*   **11**
International caps: 64*   **12**
International goals: 48*   **9**
Length of career: 10 years*   **16**
Height: 1.69 m   **18**

3. Now, challenge your friends to see who has the highest-ranking stat – the lower the number (from 1–20) the better your chances of winning. (1 = good, 20 = goofy).

Player 1

Date of birth: 24/06/87   **1**

Player 2

Date of birth: 22/05/46   **13**

4. Whoever has the lowest number is the winner – nice one! If you have the same number – you've tied.

Time to flick, choose, challenge again!

(If you land on the same game page, choose the Ultimate 20 listing opposite.)

Mash it up!

If you haven't got the same *Ultimate 20* book as your friends, you can **STILL** play — Ultimate 20 Mash Up! The rules are the same as the regular game (above), so flick and choose one of your Ultimate 20 and a stat, then read them out. Each player does this. Now read out the Ultimate 20 ranking to see whose choice is the best. Can a McLaren P1 car beat a tank? Can Genghis Khan beat a king cobra snake?

Pelé

Brazilian striker Pelé is probably the most famous footballer of all time — renowned for his spectacular goals. He was on a World Cup winning team three times.

Santos record holder

Pelé joined Santos Football Club in the city of São Paulo in 1956. He helped the team to league championships and quickly became a national footballing hero. Pelé played in 1,106 first-team matches – a Santos club record. He is still their top scorer, with 1,091 goals! Soon he was famous all over the world and his team toured internationally.

World Cup wins

Pelé first played for Brazil in 1957, when he was 16. The following year he played in the World Cup in Sweden, where he scored a hat trick in the semi-finals against France. He also scored two of the five goals in Brazil's World Cup final win against Sweden. At the end of his last World Cup, in 1970, he had scored 12 goals in his 14 World Cup matches. After three years with US team New York Cosmos, Pelé retired in 1977. In 1999, the International Federation of Football History and Statistics voted Pelé "Football Player of the Century".

Date of birth: 23/10/40   **14**
Club goals: 1,281   **1**
International caps: 91   **9**
International goals: 77   **2**
Length of career: 21 years   **3**
Height: 1.73 m   **15**

Diego Maradona

Diego Maradona was the top player of the 1980s, and despite his highs and lows, is considered one of the greatest attacking midfielders of all time. He led the Argentina team to win the World Cup in 1986.

European teams

Maradona played for a first-division side when he was just 15 years old. In 1982, he moved to Europe, playing for Barcelona in Spain and then for Napoli in Italy. He stayed at Napoli for seven years, where he helped the previously weak team to win league and cup titles.

Date of birth: 30/10/60   **8**

Club goals: 258   **9**

International caps: 91   **9**

International goals: 34   **11**

Length of career: 21 years   **3**

Height: 1.65 m   **20**

Hand of God

Aged 16, Maradona became the youngest player on the Argentina team. He went on to play in four World Cup tournaments. In the 1986 quarter-final against England, he scored the infamous "Hand of God" goal, when the ball hit his hand (not his head, as the referee thought). Argentina went on to win the World Cup, beating West Germany 3–2 in the final.

Low points

In 1991, Maradona was suspended from football after taking drugs. Then in 1994 he was sent home from the World Cup Finals after testing positive for a banned substance. Maradona retired from football in 1997.

www.biography.com/people/zinedine-zidane-9541232

Zinedine Zidane

French midfielder Zinedine Zidane was on World Cup and European Championship winning teams, and was named FIFA's "World Player of the Year" three times.

Dazzling career

Zidane began his dazzling career in 1989 at Cannes, before he transferred to Bordeaux in 1992, then to Juventus in 1996. He went on to join Real Madrid, who won the Champions League title and European Super Cup in 2002. In 1994, Zidane made his debut for France. At the 1998 World Cup finals, Zidane scored two goals as France beat Brazil 3–0 in the final. He played in two more World Cups and was awarded the FIFA World Cup Golden Ball as the best player in the 2006 World Cup.

Date of birth: 23/06/72 **5**
Club goals: 144 **14**
International caps: 108 **4**
International goals: 31 **14**
Length of career: 17 years **13**
Height: 1.85 m **5**

Golden Ball

The FIFA World Cup Golden Ball (a trophy shaped like a football) is awarded to the best player at each World Cup final. It was introduced in 1982, and was orginally called the Adidas Golden Ball. Players are voted for by members of the media.

Luís Figo

Winger Luís Figo was European Footballer of the Year in 2000, FIFA World Player of the Year in 2001 and has been capped more times than any other Portuguese player.

Date of birth: 04/11/72

Club goals: 90

International caps: 127

International goals: 32

Length of career: 20 years

Height: 1.80 m

5
17
1
13
6
10

Rival teams

In 1989, Figo played for Sporting CP – in his hometown of Lisbon – before moving to FC Barcelona. In 2000, he transferred to Barcelona's archrival, Real Madrid, for a fee that made him the most expensive footballer in the world. Barcelona fans were so angry about the move that they hurled missiles at him during Madrid-Barcelona matches – at one game, a fan threw a pig's head! In Figo's first three years at Real Madrid, the team won two league championships and a Champions League title. He played for Italian club Inter Milan from 2005 to 2009, when he ended his career.

Record-breaking caps

Figo first played for his country aged 18, in 1991. His international career included three European Championships and two World Cups – at the 2006 World Cup Figo captained Portugal to the semi-finals. He was capped a record-breaking 127 times for Portugal.

7

Michel Platini

Michel Platini was one of the outstanding players of the 1980s, a brilliant passer and free kick specialist. He played for France during three World Cup finals and was part of the team that won the 1984 European Championship.

Date of birth: 21/06/55 — 10
Club goals: 224 — 12
International caps: 72 — 15
International goals: 41 — 7
Length of career: 15 years — 14
Height: 1.78 m — 12

Player of the year

Platini began playing for his home side, Nancy, in 1972. He spent three years at Saint Etienne, before moving to the Italian team, Juventus. He was part of the Juventus team which won two league championships, a European Cup (in which he scored the winning goal) a Cup-Winners' Cup, an Intercontinental Cup and a European Super Cup. In the space of four seasons, he was voted European Footballer of the Year three times.

Euro win

The highlight of Platini's career came in 1984, when France hosted and won the European Championship. He scored a record-breaking nine goals over five matches. He was also voted best player of the championship. Platini retired in 1987, having scored over 350 goals in his professional career, 41 of them for France. In 2007, he was made president of UEFA.

Cristiano Ronaldo

Cristiano Ronaldo dos Santos Aveiro was made captain of Portugal in 2008 and started the most successful spell of his career as a forward for Real Madrid in 2009. He's considered to be one of the most skilful footballers of the 21st century.

Record transfer

After playing for Sporting CP's youth teams, Ronaldo's professional career began in 2002. The following year he moved to Manchester United, where he scored the opening goal in their FA Cup win in 2004. In 2008, after he helped Manchester United win the Champions League, he earned the FIFA World Player of the Year award. Ronaldo became the most expensive player in history in 2009 when he transferred to Real Madrid for £80 million.

Cristiano Ronaldo key facts

- Ronaldo debuted as an international player in 2003.
- He helped Portugal to fourth place in the 2006 World Cup finals.
- In 2012, he led Portugal to the semi-finals of the European Championship.
- In October 2012, he became the first athlete to receive 50 million 'Likes' on Facebook!

Date of birth: 05/02/85
Club goals: 356*
International caps: 109*
International goals: 47*
Length of career: 12 years*
Height: 1.86 m

Johan Cruyff

Johan Cruyff was one of the top players of the 1970s. He played for the Netherlands and earned the European Footballer of the Year award three times during his football career.

Date of birth: 25/04/47

Club goals: 291

International caps: 48

International goals: 33

Length of career: 20 years

Height: 1.80 m

12
6
19
12
6
10

Ajax

Cruyff began his professional career with Amsterdam's AFC Ajax when he was 17 years old. While he was there, Ajax won six league titles, four national cups and three European Championships. Cruyff moved to FC Barcelona in 1973, where he became captain. He won European Footballer of the Year Award in 1971, 1973 and 1974. From 1978, Cruyff played for teams in the USA for three years.

Managing success

Cruyff's first cap for the Netherlands came when he was 18 years old. In 1974 they lost 1–2 to West Germany in the World Cup final. Cruyff did win the tournament's Golden Ball though. In 1984 he became Ajax's manager, leading them to a Cup-Winner's Cup in 1987. Later he managed FC Barcelona, who won both the European Cup and European Super Cup in 1992.

Franz Beckenbauer

Franz Beckenbauer is perhaps Germany's greatest ever footballer. He captained his country's World Cup winning team in 1974 and was named European Footballer of the Year in 1972 and 1976.

European champion

Beckenbauer first played professionally for Bayern Münich in 1963, and became the team's captain in 1971. Under his leadership, Bayern won four national titles, as well as three European Cups, in 1974, 1975 and 1976.

Date of birth: 11/09/45

Club goals: 81

International caps: 103

International goals: 14

Length of career: 19 years

Height: 1.81 m

13
18
7
17
12
9

International star

- First played for West Germany in 1965 and became captain in 1971.
- Capped 103 times, and led West Germany to victory at Euro 1972 and the 1974 World Cup.
- Became manager of West Germany in 1984.
- One of only two people to captain and manage a World Cup winning side when West Germany won the 1990 World Cup.
- Became vice president of the German Football Federation in 1998.

Eusébio

Eusébio Ferreira da Silva, known as Eusébio, is one of the world's top players, with an astonishing goal-scoring record. He was born in Mozambique (part of Portugal at the time) and first played for Sporting Lourenço Marques.

Top scorer

In 1961 Eusébio moved to Portugal to play for Benfica in Lisbon. At the European Cup final the following year, he scored two of the match's five goals to beat Real Madrid. He earned the European Footballer of the Year title in 1965. Eusébio was the leading scorer in the Portuguese League from 1964 to 1968 and again in 1970 and 1973. He was the first player to win the Golden Boot award as Europe's top scorer in 1968. He won the award again in 1973.

Date of birth: 25/01/42 14
Club goals: 727 3
International caps: 64
International goals: 41 16
Length of career: 22 years 7
Height: 1.75 m 2
14

Golden player

Eusébio helped Portugal to third place in the 1966 World Cup, and was the top goal scorer of the tournament. Over the whole of his career, Eusébio played 715 matches and scored 727 goals. In 2003, the Portuguese Football Federation named Eusébio their Golden Player, as the best Portuguese footballer of the past 50 years.

George Best

George Best is the best-known Northern Irish player of all time, a 1960s celebrity and one of the most skilful forwards ever. He was signed by Manchester United when he was just 15 years old.

United's star player

In 1963, Best played his first professional match. His brilliant, acrobatic goal scoring quickly made him United's star player. The club were league champions in 1965 and 1967. Best won the European Footballer of the Year title in 1968, the same year United won the European Cup – the first English club to do so.

Date of birth: 22/05/46	13
Club goals: 238	10
International caps: 37	20
International goals: 9	18
Length of career: 20 years	6
Height: 1.75 m	14

Celebrity status

Best became a huge celebrity and was the first footballer to feature in British newspapers for his lifestyle rather than his football skills. He left Manchester United in 1974 and played for various clubs in Britain, Australia, Spain and the USA over the next nine years. Sadly, he suffered from alcoholism, which affected his play. He stopped playing football in 1983 and died in 2005.

Ferenc Puskás

Hungarian striker Ferenc Puskás was football's first international star. He was an Olympic gold medallist and a member of the team that won three European Cups. In 1948 he was Europe's top goal scorer.

Hungary and Spain

Puskás played for Honvéd, his hometown, and soon became famous for his deadly accurate left foot. Honvéd won five Hungarian championships between 1950 and 1955. Puskás was part of Hungary's famous Mighty Magyars team. In 1956 he was playing a match in Spain when the Hungarian Revolution broke out. Puskás defected to Spain shortly after, where he played for Real Madrid. He helped them to five league wins and three European Cups (1959, 1960 and 1966). He played for Spain in the 1962 World Cup. Puskás died in Hungary in 2006.

Date of birth: 01/04/27
Club goals: 869
International caps: 88
International goals: 83
Length of career: 23 years
Height: 1.72 m

Mighty Magyars

- Between 1950–56 the Hungary national team was called the Mighty Magyars (Golden Team) – Puskás was their top player.
- Puskás scored 83 goals in the 84 matches he played for the Mighty Magyars.
- Out of 51 games played between 1950-56, Hungary only lost one match.

Gerd Müller

German striker Gerd Müller was the first German to win European Footballer of the Year in 1970. He is regarded as one of the greatest goal scorers of all time.

Top scorer

Müller played for TSV 1861 Nördlingen, before moving to Bayern Münich in 1964. One of his new teammates was fellow superstar Franz Beckenbauer. With Müller on the team, Bayern Münich won promotion to the highest German league, and later won the German Cup four times. Müller was Bayern's top scorer for 12 consecutive years, and Europe's top scorer in 1970 and 1972. He ended his career in 1979, after two seasons in the USA.

Golden goals

Müller first played for his country, West Germany, in 1966. He was the top scorer in the 1970 World Cup, in which West Germany took third place. At Euro 1972, which West Germany won, he scored the most goals. Müller scored the winning goal in his country's win over the Netherlands in the 1974 World Cup final, after which he retired from international football, aged just 28. He had scored an incredibly impressive 68 goals in 62 international matches.

Date of birth: 03/11/45   13

Club goals: 487   4

International caps: 62   17

International goals: 68   3

Length of career: 11 years   19

Height: 1.76 m   13

Lev Yashin

Lev Yashin, from the Soviet Union, is arguably the best goalkeeper in the history of football. He is also the only keeper to have won the European Footballer of the Year award.

Dynamo

Lev Yashin's first sport was ice hockey. He was playing for his factory's football team when his talent was spotted by Dynamo Moscow. He began playing for their junior side in 1949, then for the senior team a year later. He stayed with Dynamo Moscow for 20 years and helped them to win three cups and five league titles. He became famous for his dramatic and acrobatic saves, as well as his dominance of the penalty area. Yashin won the European Footballer of the Year award in 1963.

Soviet side

Yashin began playing for the USSR national team the year after his debut with Dynamo. The team won the gold medal at the 1956 Olympics, and the European Championship in 1960 – the first one to be held. Yashin played in three World Cups and made it to the quarter-finals in 1958 and 1962, and to fourth place in 1966. He retired in 1971, and became a coach for various youth teams. Yashin died in Moscow in 1990.

Date of birth: 22/10/29	19
Club goals: 1	20
International caps: 78	14
International goals: 0	20
Length of career: 21 years	3
Height: 1.89 m	1

Bobby Charlton

English striker Bobby Charlton is often named as the greatest English footballer of all time. He played in more than 100 games for his country.

Date of birth: 11/10/37
Club goals: 277
International caps: 106
International goals: 49
Length of career: 20 years
Height: 1.73 m

16
8
6
5
6
15

United disaster

Charlton played for Manchester United throughout his career, from 1954 to 1973. In the year he joined the team, Charlton survived a plane crash in which eight other United players were killed. Despite the tragedy, United went on to play in the FA Cup final that same year. Charlton was Manchester United's captain when they became the first English club to win the European Cup in 1968.

World Cup win

Charlton first played for England in 1958, the first of over 100 caps. He was on the England team that won the World Cup in 1966, for the first and only time. He was awarded the European Footballer of the Year title the same year. After his retirement from playing, Charlton took up management and became a member of the Board of Directors for Manchester United in 1984. He was knighted in 1994 for his services to football.

Lionel Messi

Argentinian striker Lionel Messi is one of today's top players. He has been awarded FIFA's World Player of the Year four times.

Date of birth: 24/06/87 — *1*

Club goals: 342* — *11*

International caps: 83* — *12*

International goals: 37* — *9*

Length of career: 11 years* — *19*

Height: 1.69 m — *18*

Youngest scorer

As a child, Messi played for the youth team at his local top-division club in Argentina. He was so good that top clubs in South America and Europe were interested in watching him play. He moved to Spain when he was **13** years old to play in FC Barcelona's youth team, and, at the age of **17**, became the youngest player and goal scorer in Spain's football league. The following year, Barcelona won the Champions League, and in 2009 the team won three European club titles in one season. Messi became Barcelona's best-ever goal scorer in 2012, when he was just 24 years old.

Olympic gold

Messi is a national of both Argentina and Spain, but has played for Argentina since 2005. He was part of the team that went to the 2006 World Cup and was in the team that won the gold medal at the 2008 Olympics.

Wayne Rooney

Wayne Rooney became an international star while he was still a teenager. His career really took off at Premier League club Manchester United and he soon became the England national team's star forward.

Super striker

Wayne Rooney first played professionally for his local club, Everton, in 2002, when he was 16 years old. Rooney joined Manchester United in 2004, where he helped them to win four league championships, the UEFA Champions League and two League Cups.

England's youngest

In 2003, Rooney was chosen for the England national team and became the country's youngest player (though he's since been beaten by Theo Walcott) and England's youngest goal scorer. At the 2004 European Championship, Rooney played for the England squad that made it to the quarter-finals, and scored in qualifying matches for the 2010 World Cup. He's won many individual titles, including PFA Player's Player of the Year, Young Player of the Year (twice) and England Player of the Year (twice). He's the third highest paid footballer in the world, after Lionel Messi and Cristiano Ronaldo.

Date of birth: 24/10/85	2
Club goals: 141*	15
International caps: 83*	12
International goals: 36*	10
Length of career: 12 years*	16
Height: 1.76 m	13

David Beckham

English midfielder David Beckham became famous in the 1990s for shots that could bend around opposing players.

Date of birth: 02/05/75

Club goals: 97

International caps: 115

International goals: 17

Length of career: 20 years

Height: 1.83 m

Star player

When he was 11 years old, Beckham won a football contest and was taken on by Manchester United's youth squad. He started playing with the first team in 1995, and helped United win the league title and the FA Cup in his first season. Beckham was voted Young Player of the Year in 1997, and in the 1998–99 season Manchester United won the league title, the FA Cup and the European Cup. In 1999 Beckham was named UEFA's Best Midfielder and Footballer of the Year. He left Manchester United in 2003 for Real Madrid and later moved to the US to play for Los Angeles Galaxy.

World cups

Beckham played for England in three World Cups: 1998, 2002 and 2006. In 2007, he played his 100th international match. Sadly, in 2010, he injured his Achilles tendon, which meant he couldn't play in that year's World Cup. Beckham has become famous for his football skills as well as his personal life with his wife, Victoria Beckham, his fashion sense and his hair-cuts!

Marco van Basten

Dutch striker Marco van Basten was one of the world's outstanding players of the 1980s and 1990s. He won FIFA's World Player of the Year award in 1992, and the European Footballer of the Year award three times.

High score

Van Basten's professional debut came in 1982 when he played with top Dutch team Ajax. At the end of his second season with Ajax, Van Basten was the highest Dutch goal scorer. He continued to be the top goal scorer for the next three seasons, as well as helping the team win three league titles and three Dutch Cups. In 1986, he was top European goal scorer. Van Basten transferred to AC Milan in 1987, who won two European Cups (in 1989 and 1990) with him on the team.

Date of birth: 31/10/64 — **7**

Club goals: 218 — **13**

International caps: 58 — **18**

International goals: 24 — **15**

Length of career: 13 years — **15**

Height: 1.88 m — **2**

Euro semi-finals

For the Dutch national team, van Basten played in the UEFA Euro 1988 championship, where he was the top scorer, and Euro 1992 – the team made it to the semi-finals both times. Injury caused him to miss two seasons and he retired from playing in 1995, aged 30.

Bobby Moore

Bobby Moore was a super talented defensive player who captained the England side to win the country's only World Cup in 1966.

Cup winners

Moore first played professionally in 1958 for West Ham United. In 1964, West Ham won the FA Cup, with Moore as captain. The following year, Moore led the team to win the European Cup-Winners' Cup. After 15 years with West Ham, Moore transferred to Fulham FC in 1973, where he stayed for four years, followed by a final year playing professional football in Denmark.

World Cup winners

Moore first played for the England national side in 1962. He played more than 100 games for his country, 90 of them as captain. But the highlight of his international career was the 1966 World Cup. Moore captained England to a nail-biting victory over West Germany, passing the ball expertly to Geoff Hurst to score in the last few seconds of the match. After his retirement from playing football, Moore worked as a manager, a sports editor and a commentator. He died in 1993 at the age of 51.

Date of birth: 12/04/41 **14**

Club goals: 26 **19**

International caps: 108 **4**

International goals: 2 **18**

Length of career: 20 years **6**

Height: 1.83 m **8**

Ronaldo

Brazilian striker Ronaldo is one of only three players to have won the FIFA World Player of the Year award three times.

Goal average

Ronaldo played professionally from the age of 15 for Cruzeiro, scoring 58 goals in 60 matches. In 1994, he transferred to PSV Eindhoven in the Netherlands, where he scored 55 goals in 56 games. He transferred again, in 1996, to Barcelona for one season, in which Barcelona won the European Cup Winners' Cup. Ronaldo moved three more times, to clubs in Italy, Spain and Brazil.

Youngest Player of the Year

Ronaldo was first capped in 1994, at 17 years old. He didn't play in the 1994 World Cup won by Brazil, but he was on the team for Brazil's 1997 Copa America victory. In 1996, Ronaldo became the youngest player to win FIFA's World Player of the Year award, which he won twice more, as well as European Footballer of the Year. At the 2002 World Cup, he scored eight goals to help Brazil win the tournament. In 2006, he became the highest goal scorer in the history of the World Cup with 15 goals. After injuries and health issues, Ronaldo retired in 2011.

Date of birth: 18/09/76	4
Club goals: 280	7
International caps: 97	8
International goals: 62	4
Length of career: 12 years	16
Height: 1.82 m	8

Glossary

alcoholism – an addiction to alcoholic drinks

archrival – main opponent

banned substance – in sport, a substance taken to improve sporting performance

cap – a cap is awarded to a player each time he/she plays for the national team

consecutive – following one after each other

debut – first appearance

defect – leave one country or organisation for one with different values or views

FA – Football Association

FIFA – International Federation of Association Football

hat trick – one player scoring three goals in one game

league – a group of teams in a sport who play matches against each other

professional – when someone is paid to play sport

suspended – if a footballer is sent off for bad play or commits an offence, he/she will have to miss out on playing in a certain number of future matches

testing positive – when a banned substance (see above) is detected in the blood or urine of a sportsperson during routine testing

UEFA – Union of European Football Associations

Index